Pineapple Desserts

Pineapple Recipe Book with Amazing and Tasty Pineapple Recipes for Every Occasion

Delicious Pineapple Desserts

Book 3

Copyright © 2019 Brendan Fawn

All rights reserved.

ISBN: 9781087175867

Text Copyright © [Brendan Fawn]
All rights reserved. No part of this guide may be reproduced in any form without permission in writing from the publisher except in the case of brief quotations embodied in critical articles or reviews.

Legal & Disclaimer
The information contained in this book and its contents is not designed to replace or take the place of any form of medical or professional advice; and is not meant to replace the need for independent medical, financial, legal or other professional advice or services, as may be required. The content and information in this book has been provided for educational and entertainment purposes only.

The content and information contained in this book has been compiled from sources deemed reliable, and it is accurate to the best of the Author's knowledge, information, and belief. However, the Author cannot guarantee its accuracy and validity and cannot be held liable for any errors and/or omissions. Further, changes are periodically made to this book as and when needed. Where appropriate and/or necessary, you must consult a professional (including but not limited to your doctor, attorney, financial advisor or such other professional advisor) before using any of the suggested remedies, techniques, or information in this book.

Upon using the contents and information contained in this book, you agree to hold harmless the Author from and against any damages, costs, and expenses, including any legal fees potentially resulting from the application of any of the information provided by this book. This disclaimer applies to any loss, damages or injury caused by the use and application, whether directly or indirectly, of any advice or information presented, whether for breach of contract, tort, negligence, personal injury, criminal intent, or under any other cause of action.

You agree to accept all risks of using the information presented in this book.

You agree that by continuing to read this book, where appropriate and/or necessary, you shall consult a professional (including but not limited to your doctor, attorney, or financial advisor or such other advisor as needed) before using any of the suggested remedies, techniques, or information in this book.

Introduction   6

Kitchen Tools That You Will Need in Your Kitchen   7

Chapter 1   10

Pineapple Brownies   10

Pineapple and Cashews Brownies 10

Pineapple-Vanilla Brownies with Almonds   13

Pineapple and Hazelnuts Brownies with Vanilla 16

Pineapple and Cherry Brownies with Vanilla   19

Pineapple Lemon-Vanilla Brownies   22

Pineapple-Blueberry, Hazelnut and Vanilla Brownies   24

Pineapple-Cranberry, Vanilla and Walnut Brownies   27

Wild Strawberry-Pineapple Brownies   30

Pineapple-Vanilla and Pistachios Brownies   32

Pineapple, Kiwi and Banana Brownies   35

Pineapple, Mango and Peanuts Brownies   38

Pineapple, Cranberries and Peanuts Brownies   41

Pineapple, Raisins and Peanuts Brownies   44

Pineapple, Apricots and Peanuts Brownies   47

Vanilla Taste Pineapple, Banana, Orange and Peanuts Brownies   50

Chapter 2   52

Pineapple Ice Cream   52

Pineapple-Coconut Ice Cream with Blueberries 52

Pineapple-Strawberry Ice Cream 55

Pineapple-Orange Ice Cream 57

Pineapple-Lemon Ice Cream 59

Pineapple-Orange Ice Cream with Peanuts 61

Pineapple-Mango Ice Cream with Walnuts 63

Pineapple-Raspberry Ice Cream with Peanuts and Vanilla 65

Pineapple-Lemon Marmalade Ice Cream with Peanuts 68

Pineapple-Blackcurrant Ice Cream with Cashews and Milk 70

Chapter 3 72

Pineapple Jams 72

Pineapple, Cherry and Orange Jam 72

Pineapple, Cherry, Orange and Peanuts Jam 75

Pineapple-Raisins and Walnuts Jam 78

Pineapple-Blackberry Jam 80

Sugar-Free Pineapple and Raspberry Jam 83

Sugar-Free Pineapple and Lemon Jam 85

Sugar-Free Pineapple, Peanuts and Orange Jam 87

Sugar-Free Pineapple, Walnuts and Orange Jam 90

Sugar-Free Pineapple, Blackcurrant and Orange Jam 93

Sugar-Free Pineapple, Blackcurrant and Hazelnut Jam 96

Conclusion 99

Recipe Index 100

Introduction

This pineapple desserts cookbook was created to help you prepare sweet pineapple desserts. Anyone who wants to try new tastes can benefit from this pineapple recipe book.

This desserts book has various sweet pineapple recipes, such as delicious pineapple brownies, ice cream or jams. We've also added healthy, sugar-free pineapple jams. You should use your imagination because there is no limit to what you can cook when using pineapple as the main ingredient. This pineapple recipe book was created to inspire you to discover a colorful world of exotic and sweet pineapple cooking!

Kitchen Tools That You Will Need in Your Kitchen

To prepare mouth-watering pineapple brownies, jams or ice cream you will need to have the right tools in your kitchen. The following list of kitchen tools will help you.

Food scale

The food scale is the main tool. You will use it to measure any food and it will always show you the quantity of ingredients that you need for pineapple desserts.

Food processor or blender

Having a food processor or blender is important. It will help you to process, pulse, and blend various nuts, pineapple or apple cubes.

Electric hand mixer

Electric hand mixer will save your energy and of course time, especially when preparing pineapple pies where you often need to combine various ingredients and to beat the eggs.

Pot or saucepan

Having a large pot, saucepan or bowl in your kitchen is crucial for preparing pineapple desserts because you will melt, mix, combine, keep and boil all the ingredients there.

Knife sharpening stone or sharp knife

When preparing pineapple dishes you often need to chop, slice or halve some fruits. In this case, having a sharp blade in your kitchen will save you a lot of time and frustrations because you will finish cutting up your fruits much faster than you would if using a dull knife.

Baking pan

Baking pan is important because you will bake your pineapple brownies there.

Potato masher

We will need a potato masher to prepare tasty pineapple desserts and to mash pineapple, berries and other fruits.

The following chapters contain mouth-watering pineapple dessert recipes that will have your taste buds come to life!

Chapter 1

Pineapple Brownies

Pineapple and Cashews Brownies

Prep Time: 35 min. | Baking Time: 40-45 min. | Servings: 6

Ingredients:

2 cups of cashews

2 cups of pineapple, peeled and chopped or grated

3 tablespoons pure pineapple extract

10 tablespoons cocoa powder

3 eggs

10 tablespoons unsalted butter

1 cup of white sugar

1 teaspoon baking powder

spray cream

baking spray, unsalted butter or sunflower oil

How to Prepare:

1. Preheat the oven to 290°-320°Fahrenheit and roast the cashews in the oven for 10-15 minutes until lightly browned and crispy. Set aside to cool completely. Grind the cashews using a food processor.

2. Spoon the unsalted butter and sugar into a food processor and blend until there is a homogenous mass and creamy consistency.

3. Combine the cocoa powder with some sugar and mix well. Then combine the pure pineapple extract, eggs, baking powder, cocoa powder and sugar mixture and all the ingredients except for the pineapple, cashews and spray cream and blend the mixture using a food processor or an electric hand mixer until there is a smooth and creamy consistency. Mix in the pineapple and then stir in

the cashews and mix until there is a homogenous mass.

4. Preheat the oven to 290°-310° Fahrenheit and then coat the baking pan or parchment paper with the baking spray, unsalted butter or sunflower oil.

5. Spoon the sweet pineapple and cashews brownies mixture into the baking pan and bake for 40-45 minutes at 280°- 300° Fahrenheit.

6. Then cool the pineapple cashews mixture and cut it into medium size cubes. Then serve your sweet pineapple and cashews brownies with the spray cream on top. Remember that these tasty pineapple brownies should be served cold with the cup of coffee or tea.

Nutritional Information:

Calories: 149; Total fat: 27 oz; Total carbohydrates: 37 oz; Protein: 20 oz

Pineapple-Vanilla Brownies with Almonds

Prep Time: 35 min. | Baking Time: 40-45 min. | Servings: 8

Ingredients:

2 cups of almonds

5 tablespoons pure pineapple extract

2 tablespoons pure vanilla extract

2 cups of white flour

10 tablespoons cocoa powder

3 eggs

10 tablespoons unsalted butter

1 cup of white sugar

1 teaspoon baking powder

spray cream

baking spray, unsalted butter or sunflower oil

How to Prepare:

1. Preheat the oven to 290°-320°Fahrenheit and roast the almonds in the oven for 10-15 minutes until lightly browned and crispy. Set aside to cool completely. Grind the almonds using a food processor.

2. Combine the wheat flour with the eggs and mix well. Add in the unsalted butter and sugar. Spoon the mixture into a food processor and blend until there is a homogenous mass.

3. Combine the cocoa powder with the sugar and mix well. Then combine the pure pineapple extract, pure vanilla extract, eggs and flour mixture, baking powder, cocoa powder and sugar mixture and all the ingredients except for the almonds and spray cream and blend the mixture using a food processor or an electric hand mixer until there is a smooth and creamy consistency. Add in the almonds and mix until there is a homogenous mass.

4. Preheat the oven to 290°-310° Fahrenheit and then coat the baking pan or parchment paper with the baking spray, unsalted butter or sunflower oil.

5. Spoon the sweet pineapple and almonds brownies mixture into the baking pan and bake for 40-45 minutes at 280°- 300°Fahrenheit.

6. Then cool the pineapple and almonds brownies and cut them into medium size cubes. Then serve your sweet pineapple, almonds and vanilla brownies with

the spray cream on top. Remember that these tasty pineapple brownies should be served cold with the cup of coffee or tea.

Nutritional Information:

Calories: 159; Total fat: 30 oz; Total carbohydrates: 41 oz; Protein: 27 oz

Pineapple and Hazelnuts Brownies with Vanilla

Prep Time: 35 min. | Baking Time: 40-45 min. | Servings: 6

Ingredients:

2 cups of hazelnuts

2 cups of pineapple, peeled and chopped or grated

3 tablespoons pure pineapple extract

3 tablespoons pure vanilla extract

10 tablespoons cocoa powder

3 eggs

10 tablespoons unsalted butter

1 cup of white sugar

1 teaspoon baking powder

spray cream

baking spray, unsalted butter or sunflower oil

How to Prepare:

1. Preheat the oven to 290°-320°Fahrenheit and roast the hazelnuts in the oven for 10-15 minutes until lightly browned and crispy. Set aside to cool completely. Grind the hazelnuts using a food processor.

2. Spoon the unsalted butter and sugar into a food processor and blend until there is a homogenous mass and creamy consistency.

3. Combine the cocoa powder with some sugar and mix well. Then combine the pure pineapple extract, pure vanilla extract, eggs, baking powder, cocoa powder and sugar mixture and all the ingredients except for the pineapple, hazelnuts and spray cream and blend the mixture using a food processor or an electric hand mixer until there is a smooth and creamy consistency. Mix in the pineapple and then stir in the hazelnuts and mix until there is a homogenous mass.

4. Preheat the oven to 290°-310° Fahrenheit and then coat the baking pan or parchment paper with the baking spray, unsalted butter or sunflower oil.

5. Spoon the sweet pineapple and hazelnuts brownies mixture into the baking pan and bake for 40-45 minutes at 280°- 300°Fahrenheit.

6. Then cool the pineapple hazelnuts mixture and cut it into medium size cubes. Serve your sweet pineapple and hazelnuts brownies with the spray

cream on top. Remember that these tasty pineapples, hazelnuts and vanilla brownies should be served cold with the cup of coffee or tea.

Nutritional Information:

Calories: 155; Total fat: 29 oz; Total carbohydrates: 39 oz; Protein: 24 oz

Pineapple and Cherry Brownies with Vanilla

Prep Time: 20 min. | Baking Time: 45 min. | Servings: 8-10

Ingredients:

3 tablespoons pure pineapple extract

2 tablespoons pure vanilla extract

2 tablespoons pure cherry extract

1 cup of cherries, pitted

8 tablespoons cocoa powder

1 cup of unsweetened cooking chocolate (70-95%)

3 eggs

5 tablespoons coconut butter

1 cup of white sugar

1 teaspoon baking powder

banana ice cream

baking spray, unsalted butter or sunflower oil

How to Prepare:

1. Spoon the coconut butter and sugar into a food processor and blend until there is a homogenous mass and creamy consistency.

2. Mash the pitted cherries using the potato masher. Melt the cooking chocolate in a double boiler for 10-15 minutes.

3. Combine all the ingredients except for the cherries and blend the mixture using a food processor until there is a smooth and creamy consistency. Add in the cherries and then mix well until there is a homogenous mass.

4. Preheat the oven to 290°-310° Fahrenheit and then coat the baking pan with the baking spray, unsalted butter or sunflower oil.

5. Spoon the sweet pineapple, cherry and vanilla brownies mixture into the baking pan and bake for 40-45 minutes at 290°- 310°Fahrenheit.

6. Then cool the pineapple and cherry mixture with vanilla and cut it into medium size cubes. Serve your sweet pineapple brownies with the banana ice cream on top. Remember that these tasty pineapple and cherry brownies should be served cold with the cup of tea or cappuccino.

Nutritional Information:

Calories: 151; Total fat: 27 oz; Total carbohydrates: 39 oz; Protein: 21 oz

Pineapple Lemon-Vanilla Brownies

Prep Time: 30 min. | Baking Time: 55 min. | Servings: 8

Ingredients:

1 cup of pineapples, peeled and cubed

2 tablespoons pure pineapple extract

2 tablespoons lemon zest, minced

2 tablespoons pure vanilla extract

10 tablespoons cocoa powder

1 cup of unsweetened cooking chocolate (70-95%)

3 eggs

10 tablespoons unsalted butter

1 cup of white sugar

1 teaspoon baking powder

pineapple ice cream

baking spray, unsalted butter or sunflower oil

How to Prepare:

1. Spoon the unsalted butter and sugar into a food processor and blend until there is a homogenous mass and creamy consistency.

2. Melt the cooking chocolate in a double boiler for 10 or 15 minutes.

3. Combine all the ingredients except for the pineapple cubes and blend the mixture using a food processor until there is a smooth and creamy consistency. Add in the small pineapple cubes and mix until there is a homogenous mass.

4. Preheat the oven to 290°-310° Fahrenheit and then coat the baking pan or parchment paper with the baking spray, unsalted butter or sunflower oil.

5. Spoon the sweet pineapple and lemon brownies mixture into the baking pan and bake for 55 minutes at 280°- 300°Fahrenheit.

6. Then cool the pineapple and lemon mixture and cut it into medium size cubes. Serve your sweet pineapple and lemon brownies with the ice cream on top. Remember that these tasty pineapple lemon brownies should be served cold with the cup of coffee or tea.

Nutritional Information:

Calories: 150; Total fat: 26 oz; Total carbohydrates: 37 oz; Protein: 21 oz

Pineapple-Blueberry, Hazelnut and Vanilla Brownies

Prep Time: 25 min. | Baking Time: 50 min. | Servings: 8

Ingredients:

1 cup of hazelnuts, ground

3 tablespoons pure pineapple extract

1 cup of blueberries

3 tablespoons pure vanilla extract

5 tablespoons cocoa powder

1 cup of unsweetened cooking chocolate (70-95%)

3 eggs

3 tablespoons unsalted butter

5 tablespoons white sugar

1 teaspoon baking powder

pineapple ice cream

baking spray, unsalted butter or sunflower oil

How to Prepare:

1. Preheat the oven to 300°-320° Fahrenheit and roast the hazelnuts in the oven for 10 minutes until lightly browned and crispy and set aside to cool completely. Then grind the hazelnuts using a food processor.

2. Spoon the unsalted butter and sugar into a food processor and blend until there is a homogenous mass. Then stir in the hazelnuts and mix well. Mash the blueberries with the sugar using a potato masher.

3. Blend all the ingredients using a food processor or blender until there is a smooth and creamy consistency. Add in the blueberries and mix until there is a homogenous mass. Melt the cooking chocolate in a double boiler for 10 minutes and combine with all the ingredients.

4. Preheat the oven to 280°-300° Fahrenheit and then coat the baking pan with the baking spray, unsalted butter or sunflower oil.

5. Spoon the sweet pineapple-blueberry, hazelnut and vanilla brownies mixture into the baking pan and bake for 50 minutes at 300°- 320° Fahrenheit.

6. Then cool the pineapple-blueberry, hazelnut and vanilla brownies mixture and cut it into medium size squares. Then serve your tasty brownies with the pineapple ice cream on top. Remember that these delicious pineapple-blueberry hazelnut

brownies should be served cool with the cup of blueberry tea.

Nutritional Information:

Calories: 168; Total fat: 30 oz; Total carbohydrates: 42 oz; Protein: 29 oz

Pineapple-Cranberry, Vanilla and Walnut Brownies

Prep Time: 35 min. | Baking Time: 75 min. | Servings: 6

Ingredients:

2 cups of walnuts, ground

3 tablespoons pure pineapple extract

1 cup of cranberries

6 tablespoons cocoa powder

1 cup of unsweetened cooking chocolate (70-95%)

4 eggs

4 tablespoons unsalted butter

2 cups of white sugar

1 teaspoon baking powder

spray cream

baking spray, unsalted butter or sunflower oil

How to Prepare:

1. Preheat the oven to 320°-340°Fahrenheit and roast the walnuts in the oven for 10 minutes until lightly browned and crispy. Set aside to cool completely. Grind the walnuts using a food processor.

2. Spoon the unsalted butter and sugar into a food processor and blend until there is a homogenous mass. Then stir in the walnuts and mix well.

3. Blend all ingredients using a food processor or blender until there is a smooth and creamy consistency. Add in the cranberries and mix until there is a homogenous mass. Melt the cooking chocolate in a double boiler for 15-20 minutes and combine with all the ingredients.

4. Preheat the oven to 280°-300° Fahrenheit and then coat the baking pan with the baking spray, unsalted butter or sunflower oil.

5. Spoon the sweet pineapple-cranberry and walnut brownies mixture into the baking pan and bake for 55 minutes at 300°- 320° Fahrenheit.

6. Then cool the pineapple-cranberry and walnut brownies mixture and cut it into medium size squares. Then serve your tasty brownies with the spray cream or pineapple ice cream on top. Remember that these delicious brownies should be served cool with the cup of coffee.

Nutritional Information:

Calories: 170; Total fat: 32 oz; Total carbohydrates: 44 oz; Protein: 30 oz

Wild Strawberry-Pineapple Brownies

Prep Time: 10 min. | Baking Time: 50 min. | Servings: 4

Ingredients:

2 cups of wild strawberries

2 cups of pineapples, peeled and grated

3 tablespoons pure pineapple extract

1 cup of hazelnuts

6 tablespoons cocoa powder

5 tablespoons unsalted butter

1 cup of unsweetened cooking chocolate (70-95%)

6 tablespoons coconut oil

3 teaspoons baking powder

1 cup of sugar

1 teaspoon cinnamon

baking spray, unsalted butter or sunflower oil

How to Prepare:

1. Preheat the oven to 280°-300° Fahrenheit and roast the hazelnuts in the oven for 10 minutes until lightly browned and crispy, then set aside to cool completely. Mash the wild strawberries with the sugar using a potato masher and set aside.

2. Melt the cooking chocolate in a double boiler for 10-20 minutes and then stir in the other ingredients and mix well using an electric hand mixer.

3. Preheat the oven to 300°-320° Fahrenheit and then coat the baking pan with the baking spray, unsalted butter or sunflower oil.

4. Pour the mixture into the baking pan and bake it for around 40-50 minutes and then cut it into small cubes. Serve your mouth-watering mango pineapple brownies. Remember that these tasty wild strawberry-pineapple brownies should be served cold with the glass of the pineapple or orange juice.

Nutritional Information:

Calories: 174; Total fat: 34 oz; Total carbohydrates: 47 oz; Protein: 32 oz

Pineapple-Vanilla and Pistachios Brownies

Prep Time: 35 min. | Baking Time: 75 min. | Servings: 6

Ingredients:

2 cups of pistachios

3 tablespoons pure pineapple extract

3 tablespoons pure vanilla extract

6 tablespoons cocoa powder

1 cup of unsweetened cooking chocolate (70-95%)

4 eggs

4 tablespoons unsalted butter

2 cups of white sugar

1 teaspoon baking powder

pineapple ice cream

baking spray, unsalted butter or sunflower oil

How to Prepare:

1. Preheat the oven to 320°-340°Fahrenheit and roast the pistachio nuts in the oven for 10 minutes until lightly browned and crispy. Set aside to cool completely. Grind the pistachios using a food processor.

2. Spoon the unsalted butter and sugar into a food processor and blend until there is a homogenous mass. Then stir in the pistachios and mix well.

3. Blend all ingredients using a food processor or blender until there is a smooth and creamy consistency. Mix in the pure vanilla extract and pure pineapple extract, mix until there is a homogenous mass. Melt the cooking chocolate in a double boiler for 15-20 minutes and combine with all the ingredients.

4. Preheat the oven to 280°-300° Fahrenheit and then coat the baking pan with the baking spray, unsalted butter or sunflower oil.

5. Spoon the sweet pineapple-vanilla and pistachios brownies mixture into the baking pan and bake for 55 minutes at 300°- 320° Fahrenheit.

6. Then cool the pineapple-vanilla and pistachios brownies mixture and cut it into medium size squares. Then serve your tasty brownies with the spray cream or pineapple ice cream on top. Remember that these delicious brownies should be served cool with the cup of coffee.

Nutritional Information:

Calories: 175; Total fat: 35 oz; Total carbohydrates: 47 oz; Protein: 32 oz

Pineapple, Kiwi and Banana Brownies

Prep Time: 15 min. | Baking Time: 55 min. | Servings: 5

Ingredients:

2 cups of pineapples, grated

3 tablespoons pure pineapple extract

5 bananas, cubed

2 tablespoons pure banana extract

2 cups of kiwis, peeled and cubed

6 tablespoons cocoa powder

5 tablespoons unsalted butter

1 cup of unsweetened cooking chocolate (70-95%)

6 tablespoons coconut oil

3 teaspoons baking powder

1 cup of sugar

1 teaspoon cinnamon

baking spray, unsalted butter or sunflower oil

How to Prepare:

1. Mash the bananas and kiwis with the cinnamon using a potato masher.

2. Melt the cooking chocolate in a double boiler for 10 minutes and then stir in the other ingredients and mix well using an electric hand mixer.

3. Preheat the oven to 300°-320° Fahrenheit and then coat the baking pan with the baking spray, unsalted butter or sunflower oil.

4. Pour the mixture into the baking pan and bake it for around 40-50 minutes and then cut it into small cubes. Serve your delicious pineapple, kiwi and banana brownies. Remember that these tasty brownies should be served cold with the pineapple juice.

Nutritional Information:

Calories: 172; Total fat: 32 oz; Total carbohydrates: 47 oz; Protein: 29 oz

Pineapple, Mango and Peanuts Brownies

Prep Time: 25 min. | Baking Time: 60 min. | Servings: 4

Ingredients:

3 cups of pineapples, grated

3 cups of mangos, peeled and grated

1 cup of peanuts

1 teaspoon citric acid or few tablespoons lemon juice

7 tablespoons cocoa powder

5 tablespoons unsalted butter

1 cup of unsweetened cooking chocolate (70-95%)

3 eggs

1 cup of flour

5 tablespoons coconut oil

2 teaspoons baking powder

1 cup of sugar

baking spray, unsalted butter or sunflower oil

Instructions:

1. Mash the pineapple and mango with the half of the sugar using a potato masher.

2. Preheat the oven to 300°-320° Fahrenheit and roast the peanuts in the oven for 10 minutes until lightly browned and crispy, then set aside. Grind the peanuts using a food processor or blender.

3. Beat the eggs with the sugar using an electric hand mixer until the mixture becomes foamy and grows in volume at least two-three times.

4. Add the flour and beat the eggs mixture for 10 minutes more. Then mix in the baking powder. Combine all brownies ingredients and mix well.

5. Melt the cooking chocolate in a double boiler for 10 minutes and then stir in the other ingredients and mix well using a hand mixer.

6. Preheat the oven to 300°-320° Fahrenheit and then coat the baking pan with the baking spray, unsalted butter or sunflower oil.

7. Pour the brownies mixture into the baking pan and bake for around 40-50 minutes. Cut the mixture into squares and then you are free to serve your pineapple, mango and peanuts brownies. Remember that these delicious brownies should be served cold with the cup of cocoa.

Nutritional Information:

Calories: 175; Total fat: 37 oz; Total carbohydrates: 49 oz; Protein: 32 oz

Pineapple, Cranberries and Peanuts Brownies

Prep Time: 25 min. | Baking Time: 60 min. | Servings: 4

Ingredients:

3 cups of pineapples, peeled and grated

2 cups of cranberries

1 cup of peanuts

1 teaspoon citric acid or few tablespoons lemon juice

7 tablespoons cocoa powder

5 tablespoons unsalted butter

1 cup of unsweetened cooking chocolate (70-95%)

3 eggs

1 cup of flour

5 tablespoons coconut oil

2 teaspoons baking powder

1 cup of sugar

baking spray, unsalted butter or sunflower oil

Instructions:

1. Mash the pineapple and cranberries with the half of the sugar using a potato masher.

2. Preheat the oven to 300°-320°Fahrenheit and roast the peanuts in the oven for 10 minutes until lightly browned and crispy, then set aside. Grind the peanuts using a food processor or blender.

3. Beat the eggs with the sugar using an electric hand mixer until the mixture becomes foamy and grows in volume at least two-three times.

4. Add the flour and beat the eggs mixture for 10 minutes more. Then mix in the baking powder. Combine all brownies ingredients and mix well.

5. Melt the cooking chocolate in a double boiler for 10 minutes and then stir in the other ingredients and mix well using a hand mixer.

6. Preheat the oven to 300°-320° Fahrenheit and then coat the baking pan with the baking spray, unsalted butter or sunflower oil.

7. Pour the brownies mixture into the baking pan and bake for around 40-50 minutes. Cut the mixture into squares and then you are free to serve your pineapple, cranberries and peanuts brownies. Remember that these delicious brownies should be served cold with the cup of cocoa.

Nutritional Information:

Calories: 178; Total fat: 39 oz; Total carbohydrates: 51 oz; Protein: 34 oz

Pineapple, Raisins and Peanuts Brownies

Prep Time: 25 min. | Baking Time: 60 min. | Servings: 4

Ingredients:

3 cups of pineapples, peeled and grated

2 cups of raisins

2 cups of peanuts

1 teaspoon citric acid or few tablespoons lemon juice

7 tablespoons cocoa powder

5 tablespoons unsalted butter

1 cup of unsweetened cooking chocolate (70-95%)

3 eggs

1 cup of flour

5 tablespoons coconut oil

2 teaspoons baking powder

1 cup of sugar

baking spray, unsalted butter or sunflower oil

Instructions:

1. Mash the pineapple with the half of the sugar using a potato masher.

2. Preheat the oven to 300°-320°Fahrenheit and roast the peanuts in the oven for 10 minutes until lightly browned and crispy, then set aside. Grind the peanuts using a food processor or blender.

3. Beat the eggs with the sugar using an electric hand mixer until the mixture becomes foamy and grows in volume at least two-three times.

4. Add the flour and beat the eggs mixture for 10 minutes more. Then mix in the baking powder. Combine all brownies ingredients and mix well.

5. Melt the cooking chocolate in a double boiler for 10 minutes and then stir in the other ingredients and mix well using a hand mixer.

6. Preheat the oven to 300°-320° Fahrenheit and then coat the baking pan with the baking spray, unsalted butter or sunflower oil.

7. Pour the brownies mixture into the baking pan and bake for around 40-50 minutes. Cut the mixture into squares and then you are free to serve your pineapple, raisins and peanuts brownies. Remember that these delicious brownies should be served cold with the cup of cocoa.

Tip: You can pour hot, melted chocolate on top.

Nutritional Information:

Calories: 181; Total fat: 41 oz; Total carbohydrates: 52 oz; Protein: 36 oz

Pineapple, Apricots and Peanuts Brownies

Prep Time: 25 min. | Baking Time: 60 min. | Servings: 4

Ingredients:

3 cups of pineapples, peeled and grated

2 cups of apricots, dried

2 cups of peanuts

1 teaspoon citric acid or few tablespoons lemon juice

7 tablespoons cocoa powder

5 tablespoons unsalted butter

1 cup of unsweetened cooking chocolate (70-95%)

3 eggs

1 cup of flour

5 tablespoons coconut oil

2 teaspoons baking powder

1 cup of sugar

baking spray, unsalted butter or sunflower oil

Instructions:

1. Soak the apricots in the warm water for around 10-20 minutes and then chop them. Mash the pineapple with the half of the sugar using a potato masher.

2. Preheat the oven to 300°-320°Fahrenheit and roast the peanuts in the oven for 10 minutes until lightly browned and crispy, then set aside. Grind the peanuts using a food processor or blender.

3. Beat the eggs with the sugar using an electric hand mixer until the mixture becomes foamy and grows in volume at least two-three times.

4. Add the flour and beat the eggs mixture for 10 minutes more. Then mix in the baking powder. Combine all brownies ingredients and mix well.

5. Melt the cooking chocolate in a double boiler for 10 minutes and then stir in the other ingredients and mix well using a hand mixer.

6. Preheat the oven to 300°-320° Fahrenheit and then coat the baking pan with the baking spray, unsalted butter or sunflower oil.

7. Pour the brownies mixture into the baking pan and bake for around 40-50 minutes. Cut the mixture into squares and then you are free to serve your pineapple, apricots and peanuts brownies. Remember that these delicious brownies should be served cold with the cup of cocoa.

Nutritional Information:

Calories: 180; Total fat: 43 oz; Total carbohydrates: 53 oz; Protein: 35 oz

Vanilla Taste Pineapple, Banana, Orange and Peanuts Brownies

Prep Time: 30 min. | Baking Time: 60 min. | Servings: 8

Ingredients:

3 tablespoons pure pineapple extract

3 tablespoons pure banana extract

3 tablespoons orange zest, minced

1 cup of peanut butter

1 teaspoon citric acid or few tablespoons lemon juice

7 tablespoons cocoa powder

5 tablespoons unsalted butter

1 cup of unsweetened cooking chocolate (70-95%)

3 eggs

1 cup of flour

5 tablespoons coconut oil

2 teaspoons baking powder

1 cup of sugar

baking spray, unsalted butter or sunflower oil

Instructions:

1. Beat the eggs with the sugar using an electric hand mixer until the mixture becomes foamy and grows in volume at least two-three times.

2. Add the flour and beat the eggs mixture for 10 minutes more. Then mix in the baking powder. Combine all brownies ingredients and mix well.

3. Melt the cooking chocolate in a double boiler for 10 minutes and then stir in the other ingredients and mix well using a hand mixer.

4. Preheat the oven to 300°-320° Fahrenheit and then coat the baking pan with the baking spray, unsalted butter or sunflower oil.

5. Pour the brownies mixture into the baking pan and bake for around 40-50 minutes. Cut the mixture into squares and then you are free to serve your pineapple, vanilla, banana, orange and peanuts brownies. Remember that these delicious brownies should be served cold with the cup of cocoa.

Nutritional Information:

Calories: 182; Total fat: 44 oz; Total carbohydrates: 54 oz; Protein: 36 oz

Chapter 2

Pineapple Ice Cream

Pineapple-Coconut Ice Cream with Blueberries

Prep Time: 20 min. | Servings: 3

Ingredients:

3 tablespoons pure pineapple extract

1 cup of fresh blueberries

5 tablespoons shredded coconut

1 cup of unsweetened coconut milk

6 tablespoons coconut butter

1 cup of sugar

2 tablespoons pure vanilla extract

How to Prepare:

1. Mash the blueberries with the sugar using a potato masher.

2. Pulse the mashed blueberries, coconut milk, coconut butter, shredded coconut, pure pineapple extract and vanilla using a blender or food processor.

3. Spoon the mixture into the ice cream maker and process it for around 1.5 hour or according to manufacturer's instructions.

4. Spoon the pineapple-coconut mixture into the silicone molds or an ice tray.

5. Freeze the pineapple, coconut and blueberries ice cream for overnight and then serve.

Nutritional Information:

Calories: 174; Total fat: 42 oz; Total carbohydrates: 52 oz; Protein: 32 oz

Pineapple-Strawberry Ice Cream

Prep Time: 30 min. | *Servings: 5*

Ingredients:

3 tablespoons pure pineapple extract

2 tablespoons pure strawberry extract

1 cup of fresh strawberries

5 tablespoons shredded coconut

1 cup of milk

6 tablespoons coconut butter

1 cup of brown sugar

2 tablespoons pure vanilla extract

How to Prepare:

1. Mash the strawberries with the sugar using a potato masher.
2. Pulse the mashed strawberries, milk, coconut butter, shredded coconut, pure pineapple extract,

pure strawberry extract and vanilla using a blender or food processor.

3. Spoon the mixture into the ice cream maker and process it for around 1.5 hour or according to manufacturer's instructions.

4. Spoon the pineapple-strawberry mixture into the silicone molds or an ice tray.

5. Freeze the pineapple-strawberry ice cream for overnight and then serve.

Nutritional Information:

Calories: 173; Total fat: 41 oz; Total carbohydrates: 51 oz; Protein: 31 oz

Pineapple-Orange Ice Cream

Prep Time: 35 min. | *Servings: 6*

Ingredients:

1 cup of pineapple, grated

3 tablespoons pure pineapple extract

2 tablespoons orange zest, minced

5 tablespoons shredded coconut

2 cups of coconut milk

6 tablespoons coconut butter

1 cup of white sugar

2 tablespoons pure vanilla extract

How to Prepare:

1. Mash the pineapple with the sugar using a potato masher.

2. Pulse the mashed pineapple, coconut milk, coconut butter, shredded coconut, pure pineapple extract,

orange zest and vanilla using a blender or food processor.

3. Spoon the mixture into the ice cream maker and process it for around 1.5 hour or according to manufacturer's instructions.

4. Spoon the pineapple-orange mixture into the silicone molds or an ice tray.

5. Freeze the pineapple-orange ice cream for overnight and then serve.

Nutritional Information:

Calories: 172; Total fat: 42 oz; Total carbohydrates: 50 oz; Protein: 30 oz

Pineapple-Lemon Ice Cream

Prep Time: 45 min. | Servings: 4

Ingredients:

1 cup of pineapple, grated

3 tablespoons pure pineapple extract

2 tablespoons lemon zest, minced

5 tablespoons lemon juice

2 cups of coconut milk

6 tablespoons coconut butter

1 cup of white sugar

2 tablespoons pure vanilla extract

How to Prepare:

1. Mash the pineapple with the sugar using a potato masher.
2. Pulse the mashed pineapple, coconut milk, coconut butter, shredded coconut, pure pineapple extract, lemon zest, lemon juice and vanilla using a blender or food processor.
3. Spoon the mixture into the ice cream maker and process it for around 1.5 hour or according to manufacturer's instructions.
4. Spoon the pineapple-lemon mixture into the silicone molds or an ice tray.
5. Freeze the pineapple-lemon ice cream for overnight and then serve.

Nutritional Information:

Calories: 175; Total fat: 45 oz; Total carbohydrates: 51 oz; Protein: 32 oz

Pineapple-Orange Ice Cream with Peanuts

Prep Time: 55 min. | *Servings: 6*

Ingredients:

1 cup of pineapple, grated

1 cup of peanuts

3 tablespoons pure pineapple extract

2 tablespoons orange zest, minced

5 tablespoons shredded coconut

2 cups of coconut milk

6 tablespoons coconut butter

1 cup of white sugar

2 tablespoons pure vanilla extract

How to Prepare:

1. Preheat the oven to 300°-320°Fahrenheit and roast the peanuts in the oven for around 20 minutes until

lightly browned and crispy, then set aside. Grind the peanuts using a food processor or blender.

2. Mash the pineapple with the sugar using a potato masher.

3. Pulse the mashed pineapple, coconut milk, coconut butter, shredded coconut, pure pineapple extract, orange zest and vanilla using a blender or food processor. Mix in the roasted peanuts.

4. Spoon the mixture into the ice cream maker and process it for around 1.5 hour or according to manufacturer's instructions.

5. Spoon the pineapple-orange and peanuts mixture into the silicone molds or an ice tray.

6. Freeze the pineapple-orange ice cream with peanuts for overnight and then serve.

Tip: Sprinkle some peanuts on top of the ice cream and the serve.

Nutritional Information:

Calories: 175; Total fat: 45 oz; Total carbohydrates: 52 oz; Protein: 34 oz

Pineapple-Mango Ice Cream with Walnuts

Prep Time: 55 min. | *Servings: 6*

Ingredients:

1 cup of pineapple, grated

1 cup of walnuts

3 tablespoons pure pineapple extract

3 tablespoons pure mango extract

5 tablespoons shredded coconut

2 cups of coconut milk

6 tablespoons coconut butter

1 cup of white sugar

2 tablespoons pure vanilla extract

How to Prepare:

1. Preheat the oven to 300°-320°Fahrenheit and roast the walnuts in the oven for around 20 minutes until

lightly browned and crispy, then set aside. Grind the walnuts using a food processor or blender.

2. Mash the pineapple with the sugar using a potato masher.

3. Pulse the mashed pineapple, coconut milk, coconut butter, shredded coconut, pure pineapple extract, pure mango extract and vanilla using a blender or food processor. Mix in the roasted walnuts.

4. Spoon the mixture into the ice cream maker and process it for around 1.5 hour or according to manufacturer's instructions.

5. Spoon the pineapple-mango and walnuts mixture into the silicone molds or an ice tray.

6. Freeze the pineapple-mango ice cream and walnuts for overnight and then serve.

Tip: Sprinkle some walnuts on top of the ice cream and the serve.

Nutritional Information:

Calories: 176; Total fat: 46 oz; Total carbohydrates: 54 oz; Protein: 35 oz

Pineapple-Raspberry Ice Cream with Peanuts and Vanilla

Prep Time: 60 min. | *Servings: 7*

Ingredients:

1 cup of pineapple, grated

1 cup of peanuts

3 tablespoons pure pineapple extract

3 tablespoons pure raspberry extract

3 tablespoons pure vanilla extract

3 tablespoons raspberry jam

5 tablespoons shredded coconut

2 cups of coconut milk

6 tablespoons coconut butter

1 cup of white sugar

How to Prepare:

1. Preheat the oven to 300°-320°Fahrenheit and roast the peanuts in the oven for around 20 minutes until lightly browned and crispy, then set aside. Grind the peanuts using a food processor or blender.
2. Mash the pineapple with the sugar using a potato masher.
3. Pulse the mashed pineapple, coconut milk, coconut butter, shredded coconut, pure pineapple extract, pure raspberry extract, raspberry jam and vanilla using a blender or food processor. Mix in the roasted peanuts.
4. Spoon the mixture into the ice cream maker and process it for around 1.5 hour or according to manufacturer's instructions.
5. Spoon the pineapple-raspberry and peanuts mixture into the silicone molds or an ice tray.

6. Freeze the pineapple-raspberry ice cream with peanuts for overnight and then serve.

Tip: Sprinkle some peanuts on top of the ice cream and the serve.

Nutritional Information:

Calories: 177; Total fat: 47 oz; Total carbohydrates: 54 oz; Protein: 35 oz

Pineapple-Lemon Marmalade Ice Cream with Peanuts

Prep Time: 60 min. | Servings: 7

Ingredients:

1 cup of pineapple, grated

1 cup of peanuts

3 tablespoons pure pineapple extract

5 tablespoons lemon marmalade

3 tablespoons pure lemon extract

5 tablespoons shredded coconut

2 cups of coconut milk

6 tablespoons coconut butter

1 cup of white sugar

How to Prepare:

1. Preheat the oven to 300°-320°Fahrenheit and roast the peanuts in the oven for around 20 minutes until

lightly browned and crispy, then set aside. Grind the peanuts using a food processor or blender.

2. Mash the pineapple with the sugar and lemon marmalade using a potato masher.

3. Pulse the mashed pineapple and lemon marmalade, coconut milk, coconut butter, shredded coconut, pure pineapple extract and pure lemon extract, using a blender or food processor. Mix in the roasted peanuts.

4. Spoon the mixture into the ice cream maker and process it for around 2 hours or according to manufacturer's instructions.

5. Spoon the pineapple-lemon marmalade and peanuts mixture into the silicone molds or an ice tray.

6. Freeze the pineapple-lemon marmalade ice cream with peanuts for overnight and then serve.

Tip: Sprinkle some peanuts on top of the lemon ice cream and then serve with the lemon marmalade.

Nutritional Information:

Calories: 178; Total fat: 48 oz; Total carbohydrates: 55 oz; Protein: 37 oz

Pineapple-Blackcurrant Ice Cream with Cashews and Milk

Prep Time: 60 min. | Servings: 8

Ingredients:

1 cup of pineapple, grated

1 cup of cashews

1 cup of blackcurrants

3 tablespoons pure pineapple extract

2 teaspoons citric acid

2 cups of milk

6 tablespoons coconut butter

1 cup of white sugar

How to Prepare:

1. Preheat the oven to 300°-320°Fahrenheit and roast the cashews in the oven for around 20 minutes until lightly browned and crispy, then set aside. Grind the cashews using a food processor or blender.

2. Mash the pineapple with the sugar and blackcurrants using a potato masher.

3. Pulse the mashed pineapple and blackcurrants, milk, coconut butter, pure pineapple extract and citric acid, using a blender or food processor. Mix in the roasted cashews.

4. Spoon the mixture into the ice cream maker and process it for around 2 hours or according to manufacturer's instructions.

5. Spoon the pineapple-blackcurrant and cashews mixture into the silicone molds or an ice tray.

6. Freeze the pineapple-blackcurrant ice cream for overnight and then serve.

Tip: Sprinkle some cashews on top of the blackcurrant ice cream and then serve with the blackcurrant jam.

Nutritional Information:

Calories: 179; Total fat: 49 oz; Total carbohydrates: 56 oz; Protein: 38 oz

Chapter 3

Pineapple Jams

Pineapple, Cherry and Orange Jam

Prep Time: 45 min. | 7 10 oz jars

Ingredients:

5 cups of cherries, pitted

4 cups of pineapple, cubed

4 tablespoons pure pineapple extract

4 cups of oranges, peeled and cubed

3 cups of sugar

2 teaspoons citric acid

1 teaspoon vanilla

How to Prepare:

1. Preheat the oven to 180°-220° Fahrenheit and put the empty jars in the oven for around 10-15 minutes to sterilize or dry them, if you washed them.

2. Boil the pineapples, cherries and oranges with the sugar over medium heat for around 40-45 minutes, stirring all the time until the sugar dissolves. Remove the foam from the pineapple jam surface while stirring.

3. Pour some pineapple, cherry and orange jam on a plate and check if it has gelled, by pressing with the finger. If not gelled enough continue boiling and testing every 5 or 10 minutes. Remember that the pineapple jam should be thick enough to spoon it into the jars. Few minutes before the jam is ready mix in the citric acid, pure pineapple extract, and vanilla and keep stirring for a few minutes until there is a homogenous mass.

4. When the pineapple-cherry jam is ready, remove the saucepan from the heat and spoon the freshly

cooked jam into the sterilized and hot jars up to 1/5 inch from the top and only then seal the jars.

5. Then flip the jars with the pineapple, cherry and orange jam upside down or boil for around 10 minutes and then leave to cool. Remember to check the lids by pressing them with the finger. In case some of the jars with the pineapple, cherry and orange jam are unsealed, place them into the fridge or reprocess the unsealed jars.

Nutritional Information:

Calories: 75; Total fat: 12 oz; Total carbohydrates: 29 oz; Protein: 7 oz

Pineapple, Cherry, Orange and Peanuts Jam

Prep Time: 45 min. | 7 10 oz jars

Ingredients:

2 cups of peanuts

5 cups of cherries, pitted

4 cups of pineapple, cubed

4 tablespoons pure pineapple extract

4 cups of oranges, peeled and cubed

3 cups of sugar

2 teaspoons citric acid

1 teaspoon vanilla

How to Prepare:

1. Preheat the oven to 300°-320°Fahrenheit and roast the peanuts in the oven for 10 minutes until lightly browned and crispy, then set aside. Grind the peanuts using a food processor or blender.

2. Preheat the oven to 180°-220° Fahrenheit and put the empty jars in the oven for around 10-15 minutes to sterilize or dry them, if you washed them.

3. Boil the pineapples, cherries, oranges and peanuts with the sugar over medium heat for around 40-45 minutes, stirring all the time until the sugar dissolves. Remove the foam from the pineapple jam surface while stirring.

4. Pour some pineapple, cherry, orange and peanuts jam on a plate and check if it has gelled, by pressing with the finger. If not gelled enough continue boiling and testing every 5 or 10 minutes. Remember that the pineapple jam should be thick enough to spoon it into the jars. Few minutes before the jam is ready mix in the citric acid, pure pineapple extract, and vanilla and keep stirring for a few minutes until there is a homogenous mass.

5. When the pineapple and peanuts jam is ready, remove the saucepan from the heat and spoon the freshly cooked jam into the sterilized and hot jars up to 1/5 inch from the top and only then seal the jars.

6. Then flip the jars with the pineapple, cherry, orange and peanuts jam upside down or boil for around 10 minutes and then leave to cool. Remember to check the lids by pressing them with the finger. In case some of the jars with the pineapple, cherry, orange and peanuts jam are unsealed, place them into the fridge or reprocess the unsealed jars.

Nutritional Information:

Calories: 79; Total fat: 15 oz; Total carbohydrates: 32 oz; Protein: 9 oz

Pineapple-Raisins and Walnuts Jam

Prep Time: 50 min. | 7-8 10 oz jars

Ingredients:

2 cups of walnuts

10 cups of pineapple, cubed

3 tablespoon pure pineapple extract

2 tablespoons pure vanilla extract

4 cups of raisins

7 cups of sugar

How to Prepare:

1. Preheat the oven to 300°-320°Fahrenheit and roast the walnuts in the oven for 10 minutes until lightly browned and crispy, then set aside. Grind the walnuts using a food processor or blender. Soak the raisins in the warm water for around 10 minutes.

2. Preheat the oven to 180°-210° Fahrenheit and put the empty jars in the oven for around 15 minutes to sterilize or dry them.

3. Boil the pineapples, raisins, walnuts and sugar over medium heat for around 45-50 minutes, stirring all the time until the sugar dissolves. Skim the foam from the pineapple jam surface while stirring.

4. Pour some pineapple-raisins jam on a plate and check if it has gelled, by pressing with the finger. If not gelled enough continue boiling and testing every five or ten minutes. Remember that the pineapple raisins jam should be thick enough to spoon it into the jars. Five minutes before the jam is ready mix in the pure vanilla extract and pure pineapple extract.

5. When the pineapple-raisins jam is ready, remove the saucepan from the heat and spoon the freshly cooked jam into the sterilized and hot jars up to 1/4 inch from the top and only then seal the jars.

6. Then flip the jars with the pineapple-raisins jam upside down or boil for around 10 minutes and then leave to cool. Remember to check the lids by pressing them with the finger. In case some of the jars with the pineapple-raisins jam are unsealed, place them into the fridge or reprocess the unsealed jars.

Nutritional Information:

Calories: 81; Total fat: 18 oz; Total carbohydrates: 34 oz; Protein: 10 oz

Pineapple-Blackberry Jam

Prep Time: 50 min. | 6-7 11 oz jars

Ingredients:

2 pineapples, peeled and cubed

5 cups of blackberries

5 cups of sugar

4 teaspoons pure vanilla extract

1 teaspoon citric acid

How to Prepare:

1. Preheat the oven to 170°-200° Fahrenheit and put the empty jars in the oven for around 10-15 minutes to sterilize them.

2. Place the blackberries and pineapples into a big pot and spoon the sugar on top. Leave for at least 1 hour unrefrigerated at room temperature or place in the fridge for overnight.

3. Then boil the pineapples and blackberries over medium heat for around 25 minutes, stirring all the time until the sugar dissolves. Remove the scum from the jam surface. Then reduce the heat and continue to boil for around 25 minutes.

4. Few minutes before the pineapple and blackberry jam is ready mix in the pure vanilla extract and citric acid, and keep stirring until the jam has gelled and thickened. Pour some jam on a plate and check if gelled, pressing it with the finger, if not continue boiling and testing every 10 minutes. Remember that the pineapple and blackberry jam should be thick enough to spoon it into the jars.

5. Remove the saucepan with the pineapple and blackberry jam from the heat and spoon the freshly cooked jam into the sterilized and hot jars up to 1/5 inch from the top.

6. Seal the jars and then turn them upside down. Leave them for overnight to cool completely and only then turn them back.

7. Or you can process the jars in the water bath. Boil the jars for around 10 minutes and then leave to cool. It is important to remember to check the lids by pressing them with the finger. In case some of the jars with the pineapple and blackberry jam are unsealed, place them into the fridge or reprocess the unsealed jars.

Nutritional Information:

Calories: 65; Total fat: 7 oz; Total carbohydrates: 18 oz; Protein: 5 oz

Sugar-Free Pineapple and Raspberry Jam

Prep Time: 55 min. | 9-10 10 oz jars

Ingredients:

10 cups of pineapples, peeled and cubed

5 cups of raspberries

1 tablespoon pure pineapple extract

1 tablespoon pure raspberry extract

4 tablespoons granulated erythritol

2 tablespoons liquid stevia

4 teaspoons citric acid

How to Prepare:

1. Preheat the oven to 180°-200° Fahrenheit and put the empty jars in the oven for around 5-10 minutes to sterilize or dry them, if you washed them.

2. Boil the pineapples and raspberries with the erythritol over medium heat for around 35 minutes, stirring all the time until the erythritol dissolves.

Don't forget to skim the foam from the jam surface while boiling. Keep stirring until the pineapple jam has thickened and gelled. Spoon some pineapple jam on a plate and check if it has gelled, by pressing with the finger. If not continue boiling and testing every 5 or 10 minutes. Remember that the pineapple jam should be thick enough to spoon it into the jars.

3. Five minutes before the jam is ready add in the liquid stevia, pure pineapple extract, pure raspberry extract and citric acid and remove the saucepan with the fruits from the heat to spoon freshly cooked, sugar-free pineapple jam into the sterilized and hot jars up to 1/5 inch from the top and then seal the jars.

4. Flip the jars with the sugar-free pineapple and raspberry jam upside down or boil them for around 10 minutes and then leave to cool. Remember to check the lids by pressing them with the finger. In case some of the jars with the sugar-free jam are unsealed, place them into the fridge or reprocess the unsealed jars.

Nutritional Information:

Calories: 68; Total fat: 19 oz; Total carbohydrates: 32 oz; Protein: 12 oz

Sugar-Free Pineapple and Lemon Jam

Prep Time: 55 min. | 9-10 10 oz jars

Ingredients:

10 cups of pineapples, peeled and cubed

4 tablespoons lemon zest, minced

1 lemon, cubed

1 tablespoon pure pineapple extract

4 tablespoons granulated erythritol

2 tablespoons liquid stevia

How to Prepare:

1. Preheat the oven to 180°-200° Fahrenheit and put the empty jars in the oven for around 5-10 minutes to sterilize or dry them, if you washed them.

2. Boil the pineapples and lemon with the erythritol over medium heat for around 35-40 minutes, stirring all the time until the erythritol dissolves. Don't forget to skim the foam from the jam surface while boiling. Keep stirring until the pineapple jam has thickened and gelled. Spoon some pineapple

and lemon jam on a plate and check if it has gelled, by pressing with the finger. If not continue boiling and testing every 5 or 10 minutes. Remember that the pineapple jam should be thick enough to spoon it into the jars.

3. Five minutes before the jam is ready add in the liquid stevia, lemon zest, and pure pineapple extract and remove the saucepan with the fruits from the heat to spoon freshly cooked, sugar-free pineapple jam into the sterilized and hot jars up to 1/5 inch from the top and then seal the jars.

4. Flip the jars with the sugar-free pineapple and lemon jam upside down or boil them for around 10 minutes and then leave to cool. Remember to check the lids by pressing them with the finger. In case some of the jars with the sugar-free jam are unsealed, place them into the fridge or reprocess the unsealed jars.

Nutritional Information:

Calories: 67; Total fat: 21 oz; Total carbohydrates: 38 oz; Protein: 16 oz

Sugar-Free Pineapple, Peanuts and Orange Jam

Prep Time: 55 min. | 9-10 10 oz jars

Ingredients:

10 cups of pineapples, peeled and cubed

2 ripe oranges, peeled and cubed

4 tablespoons orange zest, minced

1 cup of peanuts

1 tablespoon pure pineapple extract

4 tablespoons granulated erythritol

2 tablespoons liquid stevia

How to Prepare:

1. Preheat the oven to 180°-200° Fahrenheit and put the empty jars in the oven for around 5-10 minutes to sterilize or dry them, if you washed them.

2. Then preheat the oven to 300°-320°Fahrenheit and roast the peanuts in the oven for 10 minutes until lightly browned and crispy, then set aside. Grind the peanuts using a food processor or blender.

3. Boil the pineapples and oranges with the erythritol over medium heat for around 35-40 minutes, stirring all the time until the erythritol dissolves. Don't forget to skim the foam from the jam surface while boiling. Keep stirring until the pineapple jam has thickened and gelled. Spoon some pineapple and orange jam on a plate and check if it has gelled, by pressing with the finger. If not continue boiling and testing every 5 or 10 minutes. Remember that the pineapple jam should be thick enough to spoon it into the jars.

4. Five minutes before the jam is ready add in the liquid stevia, orange zest, peanuts, and pure pineapple extract and remove the saucepan with the fruits from the heat to spoon freshly cooked, sugar-free pineapple jam into the sterilized and hot jars up to 1/5 inch from the top and then seal the jars.

5. Flip the jars with the sugar-free pineapple and orange jam upside down or boil them for around 10 minutes and then leave to cool. Remember to check the lids by pressing them with the finger. In case some of the jars with the sugar-free jam are unsealed, place them into the fridge or reprocess the unsealed jars.

Nutritional Information:

Calories: 69; Total fat: 22 oz; Total carbohydrates: 40 oz; Protein: 19 oz

Sugar-Free Pineapple, Walnuts and Orange Jam

Prep Time: 55 min. | 9-10 10 oz jars

Ingredients:

10 cups of pineapples, peeled and cubed

2 ripe oranges, peeled and cubed

4 tablespoons orange zest, minced

2 cups of walnuts

1 tablespoon pure pineapple extract

4 tablespoons granulated erythritol

2 tablespoons liquid stevia

How to Prepare:

1. Preheat the oven to 180°-200° Fahrenheit and put the empty jars in the oven for around 5-10 minutes to sterilize or dry them, if you washed them.

2. Then preheat the oven to 300°-320° Fahrenheit and roast the walnuts in the oven for 10 minutes until

lightly browned and crispy, then set aside. Grind the walnuts using a food processor or blender.

3. Boil the pineapples and oranges with the erythritol over medium heat for around 45 minutes, stirring all the time until the erythritol dissolves. Don't forget to skim the foam from the jam surface while boiling. Keep stirring until the pineapple jam has thickened and gelled. Spoon some pineapple and orange jam on a plate and check if it has gelled, by pressing with the finger. If not continue boiling and testing every 5 or 10 minutes. Remember that the pineapple jam should be thick enough to spoon it into the jars.

4. 5 minutes before the jam is ready add in the liquid stevia, orange zest, walnuts, and pure pineapple extract and remove the saucepan with the fruits from the heat to spoon freshly cooked, sugar-free pineapple jam into the sterilized and hot jars up to 1/5 inch from the top and then seal the jars.

5. Flip the jars with the sugar-free pineapple and orange jam upside down or boil them for around 10 minutes and then leave to cool. Remember to check the lids by pressing them with the finger. In case some of the jars with the sugar-free jam are unsealed, place them into the fridge or reprocess the unsealed jars.

Nutritional Information:

Calories: 70; Total fat: 24 oz; Total carbohydrates: 42 oz; Protein: 21 oz

Sugar-Free Pineapple, Blackcurrant and Orange Jam

Prep Time: 55 min. | 10-12 10 oz jars

Ingredients:

10 cups of pineapples, peeled and cubed

8 cups of blackcurrants

2 ripe oranges, peeled and cubed

4 tablespoons orange zest, minced

2 cups of cashews

1 tablespoon pure pineapple extract

4 tablespoons granulated erythritol

2 tablespoons liquid stevia

How to Prepare:

1. Preheat the oven to 190°-210° Fahrenheit and put the empty jars in the oven for around 5-10 minutes to sterilize or dry them, if you washed them.

2. Then preheat the oven to 280°-300°Fahrenheit and roast the cashews in the oven for 10 minutes until

lightly browned and crispy, then set aside. Grind the cashews using a food processor or blender.

3. Boil the pineapples, blackcurrants and oranges with the erythritol over medium heat for around 45 minutes, stirring all the time until the erythritol dissolves. Don't forget to skim the foam from the jam surface while boiling. Keep stirring until the pineapple jam has thickened and gelled. Spoon some pineapple and blackcurrants jam on a plate and check if it has gelled, by pressing with the finger. If not continue boiling and testing every 5 or 10 minutes. Remember that the pineapple jam should be thick enough to spoon it into the jars.

4. 5 or 10 minutes before the jam is ready add in the liquid stevia, orange zest, cashews, and pure pineapple extract and remove the saucepan with the fruits from the heat to spoon the freshly cooked, sugar-free pineapple jam into the sterilized and hot jars up to 1/5 inch from the top and then seal the jars.

5. Flip the jars with the sugar-free pineapple and blackcurrants jam upside down or boil them for around 10 minutes and then leave to cool. Remember to check the lids by pressing them with the finger. In case some of the jars with the sugar-free jam are unsealed, place them into the fridge or reprocess the unsealed jars.

Nutritional Information:

Calories: 75; Total fat: 25 oz; Total carbohydrates: 44 oz; Protein: 22 oz

Sugar-Free Pineapple, Blackcurrant and Hazelnut Jam

Prep Time: 55 min. | 10-12 10 oz jars

Ingredients:

10 cups of pineapples, peeled and cubed

10 cups of blackcurrants

2 cups of hazelnuts

1 tablespoon pure pineapple extract

5 oz tablespoons liquid erythritol

3 tablespoons liquid stevia

2 teaspoons citric acid

How to Prepare:

1. Preheat the oven to 190°-210° Fahrenheit and put the empty jars in the oven for around 15 minutes to sterilize or dry them, if you washed them.

2. Then preheat the oven to 270°-290°Fahrenheit and roast the hazelnuts in the oven for 10 minutes until lightly browned and crispy, then set aside, grind the hazelnuts using a food processor.

3. Boil the pineapples and blackcurrants with the erythritol over medium heat for around 45 minutes, stirring all the time. Don't forget to skim the foam from the jam surface while boiling. Keep stirring until the pineapple jam has thickened and gelled. Spoon some pineapple and blackcurrants jam on a plate and check if it has gelled, by pressing with the finger. If not continue boiling and testing every 5 or 10 minutes. Remember that the pineapple jam should be thick enough to spoon it into the jars.

4. 5 or 10 minutes before the jam is ready add in the liquid stevia, hazelnuts, and pure pineapple extract and remove the saucepan with the fruits and berries from the heat to spoon the freshly cooked, sugar-free pineapple jam into the sterilized and hot jars up to 1/5 inch from the top and then seal the jars.

5. Flip the jars with the sugar-free pineapple and blackcurrants jam upside down or boil them for around 10 minutes and then leave to cool. Remember to check the lids by pressing them with the finger. In case some of the jars with the sugar-free pineapple and blackcurrant jam are unsealed, place them into the fridge or reprocess the unsealed jars.

Nutritional Information:

Calories: 77; Total fat: 26 oz; Total carbohydrates: 45 oz; Protein: 23 oz

Conclusion

Thank you for buying this pineapple desserts cookbook. I hope it was able to help you to prepare tasty pineapple brownies, ice creams and jams. We've added few interesting and healthy recipes with the sugar-free pineapple jams

If you've enjoyed this book, I'd greatly appreciate if you could leave an honest review on Amazon.

Reviews are very important to us authors, and it only takes a minute for you to post.

Your direct feedback could be used to help other readers to discover the advantages of pineapple desserts!

Thank you again and I hope you have enjoyed this book

Recipe Index

Almonds (13), Apricots (47), Banana (35, 50), Blackberry (80), Blackcurrant (70, 93, 96), Blueberry (24), Cashews (10, 70), Cherry (19, 72, 75), Cranberry (27), Hazelnuts (16, 97), Kiwi (35), Lemon (22, 59, 68, 85), Mango (38, 63), Milk (70), Orange (50, 57, 61, 72, 75, 87, 90, 93), Peanuts (38, 41, 44, 47, 50, 61, 65, 68, 75, 87), Pistachios (32), Raisins (44, 78), Raspberry (65, 83), Strawberry (30, 55), Vanilla (13, 16, 19, 22, 24, 27, 32, 50, 65), Walnuts (63, 78, 90), Wild Strawberry (30)

Printed in Great Britain
by Amazon